Violence in the Media

Perspectives on Violence

by Gus Gedatus

Consultant:
Dr. Michael Obsatz
Associate Professor of Sociology
Macalester College, St. Paul, Minnesota

LifeMatters
an imprint of Capstone Press
Mankato, Minnesota

LifeMatters Books are published by Capstone Press
PO Box 669 • 151 Good Counsel Drive • Mankato, Minnesota 56002
http://www.capstone-press.com

Printed in the United States of America

Library of Congress Cataloging-in-Publication Data
Gedatus, Gustav Mark.
     Violence in the Media / by Gus Gedatus.
         p.   cm. — (Perspectives on violence)
     Includes bibliographical references and index.
     Summary: Describes how violence in the media has changed over the years, the false ideas and messages it promotes, theories about its effects, and how one may resist its message.
     ISBN 0-7368-0425-0 (book) — ISBN 0-7368-0439-0 (series)
     1. Violence in mass media—Juvenile literature. 2. Mass media—Influence—Juvenile literature.
     [1. Violence in mass media. 2. Mass media—Influence.] I. Title. II. Series.
     P96.V5 G39 2000
     303.6—dc21   99-049849
                                                        CIP

Staff Credits
Rebecca Aldridge, Charles Pederson, editors; Adam Lazar, designer; Jodi Theisen, photo researcher

Photo Credits
Cover: PNI/©StockByte, large; ©Capstone Press/Adam Lazar, small
International Stock/©Stephen B. Myers, 7; ©Bob Firth, 11; ©Bobbe Wolf, 12, 35; ©Scott Barrow, 17; ©George Ancona, 21; ©James Davis, 25; ©Patric Ramsey, 33; ©Michael Paras, 39; ©John Michael, 42; ©O'Brien, 55
Visuals Unlimited/©John D. Cunningham, 28; ©Jeff Greenberg, 47, 58; ©Maureen Burkhart, 51; ©T. C. Malhotra, 57

A 0 9 8 7 6 5 4 3 2 1

Table of Contents

1	Media Violence: Then and Now	4
2	Media: Negative Ideas and Messages	14
3	Media: Positive Effects and Images	22
4	Is Violence "Good News"?	30
5	Film and TV Violence	36
6	Violence in Music and Video Games	44
7	Dealing With Media Violence	52
	Glossary	60
	For More Information	61
	Useful Addresses and Internet Sites	62
	Index	63

Chapter
Overview

- Media violence has been a concern for many years.

- The media have always influenced people.

- TV violence has increased since 1950.

- Canada has taken steps to regulate media violence.

- Ratings and censorship are topics of debate.

Chapter 1

Media Violence: Then and Now

The year was 1925. Elizabeth was 14. She had heard about the

ELIZABETH, AGE 14

"moving pictures" ever since she was a little girl. Today her parents were finally taking her to the theater to see her first movie, *The Big Parade*.

The movie was not about a real parade. It was a love story that took place during a war. Some battle scenes in the movie showed how awful war can be. Elizabeth covered her eyes during most of those parts. The movie frightened and saddened her. It also made her happy and teary during the romantic parts. She couldn't wait until the next time that she could see a movie. However, maybe next time she could see a picture without so much killing.

What Are Modern Media?

The media of the past consisted mainly of books, magazines, and newspapers. We still have these forms of media. However, media today include a lot more than in the past. Films, TV, radio, recorded music, videotapes, and video games are included now, too. This book describes the use of violence in film, TV, music, and video games. These are sometimes called mass media because they reach many people at the same time.

When people read newspapers or other printed material, they form mental images of the people, places, and events described. Those images may or may not be graphic, or vividly detailed. How real the images seem depends on the person's imagination and the description given. Film, TV, music, videos, and video games often show graphic images. People don't have to use their imagination as much.

The Influence of the Media

Since the first plays and newspapers, the media have affected people. For example, since the 1600s, people have seen William Shakespeare's plays. From that time until today, people quote his words in their daily life. After Benjamin Franklin published *Poor Richard's Almanack* in 1732, many Americans began to use his witty sayings. Horror novels of the 1800s such as *Frankenstein* and *Dracula* have fascinated readers while perhaps giving them bad dreams.

As radio, TV, and film brought messages to more people, the media's power became more apparent. There are many examples of that power.

Actor Clark Gable took off his shirt in the 1934 film *It Happened One Night.* Contrary to the custom of that time, Gable was not wearing a T-shirt. For months following the movie's release, T-shirt sales in the United States decreased.

Orson Welles aired the radio program *War of the Worlds* in 1938. The broadcast caused many people to believe Martians were attacking Earth.

After seeing a shower murder scene in the film *Psycho,* many people feared taking a shower.

The 1970s film *Jaws* frightened many swimmers with its story about a killer shark.

Wayne's World was released in the early 1990s. Afterwards, many people used the same phrases as the characters in the film.

"Surveys have proved that violence on the screen is increasing, and though it is not at the root of our problems, it is not helping them either."
—Professor Jo Groebel, University of Utrecht, the Netherlands

There is a lot of violence in the world today. People want to know why. Media violence may be one contributing factor.

Early Concerns About Film and TV Violence

In 1903, a cowboy in the silent film *The Great Train Robbery* fired his gun, point-blank, at the audience. A strong public outcry, or loud complaint, occurred over the scene. In 1922, the Motion Picture Association of America (MPAA) set standards for acceptable activities in film. The MPAA abandoned the code by 1968 and began a new movie rating system. This system judged which films were appropriate for certain age groups. The following chart lists the current rating system.

Movie Rating System

Rating	What it stands for	Who should see the movie?
G	General audiences	The movie is suitable for all ages.
PG	Parental guidance suggested	Some material may not be suitable for children.
PG-13	Parental guidance suggested for children under 13	Some material may not be suitable for children younger than 13.
R	Restricted	A parent or adult guardian must accompany anyone younger than 17.
NC-17	No children under 17	No one younger than 17 admitted.

"Congress shall make no law . . . abridging the freedom of speech or of the press."—First Amendment to the U.S. Constitution

Cam-ran's family moved to Canada from Thailand when

CAM-RAN, AGE 14

Cam-ran was 12. He likes his school and has learned a lot of French and English. His family is adjusting to life in Montreal.

Cam-ran watches a lot of TV and films. The more Cam-ran watches, the more frightened he becomes. The news stories he sees are much like the movies and cop shows he watches. At times it's hard to tell what is real and what isn't. Sometimes Cam-ran thinks that moving to North America wasn't a good idea. His family felt in danger in their homeland. However, the danger seems even worse here.

The U.S. Congress investigated TV in the 1950s. It found that 16 percent of prime time programming featured violence and crime. Prime time is usually considered to be in the evening. It is the time when the greatest number of people watch TV. By 1961, the amount of prime time violence had increased to 50 percent. By 1990, 70 to 80 percent of prime time shows contained violence or the threat of violence.

Canada and TV Violence

In 1990, the Canadian Radio-television and Telecommunications Commission (CRTC) studied TV violence and real violence. One study reviewed the results of 200 scientific studies on the subject. Another study reviewed actions other countries had taken regarding TV violence. The CRTC concluded that both studies showed a link between TV violence and violence in real life.

A Canadian citizens' request prompted ongoing research into how to handle TV violence. The Canadian Broadcaster's Association agreed to a coding system for TV programming. The coding system has been moderately successful, together with help from parents, in overseeing their children's viewing.

Censorship and Monitoring

Many people want to limit the amount of violence that appears in the media. However, in the United States, the First Amendment to the U.S. Constitution guarantees rights of free expression. Section Two of the Charter of Rights and Freedoms guarantees freedom of expression in Canada. Many groups who defend freedom of expression often oppose any attempt to censor the media. To censor means to remove content because some people find it offensive.

Some people feel that TV and movie ratings are a form of censorship. Other people believe that ratings educate, inform, and help caregivers make suitable choices for their children. Today, many makers of music recordings and video games voluntarily rate how violent their products are. People still debate rating and regulation systems and whether they are censorship.

Points to Consider

Do you think that modern media are different from media of the past? Why or why not?

Which type of media do you think is most violent? Which is least violent? Explain.

Explain some ways the media have influenced you.

Do you approve of censoring the media? Why or why not?

Chapter Overview

Media violence is only one factor that contributes to violent behavior.

Research shows that TV and film violence does affect children negatively. Exposure to this violence can increase aggressive behavior. It also can cause fear of the world and make children less sensitive to violence.

TV and film can present an inaccurate idea of what is normal. They also can give an inaccurate image of how women and men behave.

Chapter 2

Media: Negative Ideas and Messages

Violence is a learned behavior. Media violence can affect people in ways that contribute to violent behavior. However, the following factors may contribute to violent behavior, too:

Lack of empathy, or the ability to understand how excitement, fear, or pain may affect someone

Lack of a moral code, or a clear sense of right and wrong

Inability to see the results of one's own behaviors

FAST FACT

Studies show most middle school students spend more time watching TV than they spend with parents or teachers.

Boredom

No sense of purpose

Anger and a desire to get even for real or imagined wrongs

Peer pressure

Need for attention or respect

Feelings of low self-worth

Abuse or neglect during childhood

Witnessing violence at home or in the community

Easy access to weapons

Research Results

Media violence has a greater negative effect on children than on adults. You are not a child, but you may know or love children. You may have children of your own. You may want to know how media violence could affect them. Research during the past 40 years shows that TV and film violence can affect children in the following ways.

Children may develop aggressive behaviors and attitudes.
This happens most often when attractive characters commit
violent acts, show no guilt, and go unpunished.

**Media violence can create fearful or negative attitudes in
children about the real world.** Children may believe that
violence is more common than it really is. Fear of being a
victim is its own type of violence. It can affect people's
mental and physical health.

**Media violence can desensitize children to real-world
violence.** Real-world violence may not as easily disturb
children. They may often see violence as an acceptable way
to handle a problem. The emotional regret of being violent
tends to lessen.

**Media violence teaches that there are no nonviolent ways
to solve problems.**

A False View of the World

TV often shows people behaving in certain ways or experiencing
particular situations. These things may seem to happen a lot on
TV. However, that does not necessarily mean these things often
happen in the real world.

The average young person watches about 27 hours of TV a week. By age 18, he or she will have seen 40,000 killings and 200,000 acts of violence.

For instance, many people in the 1970s watched the TV situation comedy *The Brady Bunch.* Nothing serious ever happened on the show. Father gave wise advice and went to work. Mother stayed home and looked pretty. Their children played games and got along well except for occasional teasing. The maid happily cooked and cleaned. Many viewers may have thought that this was how most people lived. Some viewers may have wondered what was wrong with their own family. Their own life seemed more complicated. They had problems that couldn't be solved in 30 minutes.

A 1997 study looked at 18 hours of TV broadcast on 10 channels. During this time, there were 1,846 acts of violence. These acts included deaths, assaults, gunfire, fights, and threats with weapons. That is more than 100 violent acts per hour. Yet most people don't see 100 real-life acts of violence in an hour.

TV Guide magazine conducted a survey of daytime TV soap operas. In these programs, 96 percent of the characters who have sex are not married. Often, characters have unprotected sex with many partners. Unprotected sex is sexual behavior that isn't protected from disease or pregnancy. No surveys show that people have this much sex in the United States, Canada, or anywhere else. However, the amount of unprotected sex viewers see may lead them to believe it is common.

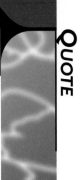
"All television is educational. The question is, what does it teach?"—Nicholas Johnson, former head of the U.S. Federal Communications Commission

These examples show that TV presents a false and inaccurate view of real life. Yet viewers, especially younger viewers, may believe that TV reflects real life.

KERRY, AGE 17

Kerry sometimes feels awkward and unattractive. It's hard to accept herself as she is when she sees the female characters on TV and in movies. They look beautiful and elegant. They are thin. Their skin is flawless. Their hair shines. Kerry believes she is nothing like that.

Kerry has had only one boyfriend, Bill. He broke up with her a month ago. Kerry thinks that if she looked and acted like the women on TV, Bill would still be her boyfriend. She wonders if she needs to lose weight or dye her hair a different color.

Harmful Images of Females and Males

Many people believe that certain TV programs and films hurt how females are viewed. These characters are usually pretty and seem concerned mainly with hairstyles, makeup, clothing, and boyfriends. However, they often don't actually think much or do much. The characters who get things done on most TV shows are males. Females often do not have the same power as males, and they may be victims of males. Female characters who do have power often are mean and controlling.

TV and films also can hurt how males are viewed. Many male movie and TV characters' actions promote the idea that real men settle arguments by fighting. Male characters rarely sit down to work out a compromise. Particularly in film, males often get out of difficult situations by using force or weapons. Young people receive the message that using violence is normal for males.

These images are harmful stereotypes of males and females. These are overly simple ideas of what a person or group is like. Stereotypes make it difficult for people to view others as individual human beings.

JOSEPH, AGE 14

Joseph felt depressed, so he went to see the school counselor. "I feel like a germ," he told Ms. Edelstein, the counselor. "My father says I'm a wimp because I don't fight back when people tease me. He even takes me to wrestling matches and action movies. He thinks it will help me learn to be more of a man."

"Fighting doesn't make you a man," Ms. Edelstein commented.

"The other night, at a movie, I started crying. I couldn't stand the sight of all the blood. My dad laughed at me and called me a baby. What's wrong with me?" Joseph asked.

"There's nothing wrong with you, Joseph. Everyone has feelings. Even your dad. You don't have to be ashamed of yours," Ms. Edelstein said.

Points to Consider

How might media violence affect children?

Do you think TV programs and movies show reality? Why or why not?

Do you think films or TV have affected your view of females' and males' roles? Why or why not?

Do you compare yourself to characters in the media? How do you think this affects the way you think of yourself?

Chapter Overview

- Many TV programs and films have shattered stereotypes and presented positive role models.

- Many TV programs and films make people aware of social issues.

- Media violence that shows the effects of hurting people can serve a positive purpose.

- TV has helped find many missing and abused children.

- TV programs can be educational.

Chapter 3

Media: Positive Effects and Images

Breaking Down Stereotypes

Many recent TV programs and films have helped break down stereotypes. *Over Easy* is one such show. It gives young people a more positive look at aging. Here are some other examples.

The Cosby Show features a father who is smart and sensitive to his children.

Chicago Hope, ER, and *The Practice* have shown successful women in nontraditional gender roles.

"The power of *Schindler's List* lies not only in seeing the faces of the victims, but also the perpetrators."
— Owen Gleiberman, movie critic, speaking of this movie that deals with the Holocaust

Dealing With Issues

TV programs and films have shed light on important social concerns. They have covered topics such as coping with AIDS and breast cancer. They have dealt with the death of loved ones. Many TV shows, news programs, and films have addressed abusive marriages and the dangers of drug and alcohol abuse. These kinds of programs educate viewers.

Some violence in TV programs and films can be used to challenge viewers. These media sometimes ask people to consider issues from the past or the current world. For instance, *Saving Private Ryan* and *The Thin Red Line* look at human suffering in wartime. The film *Dead Man Walking* shows a strong woman who speaks out against the death penalty. *Life Is Beautiful* counters the horrors of the Holocaust with humor. The Holocaust occurred during World War II when Adolf Hitler and the Nazis murdered 6 million European Jews and others.

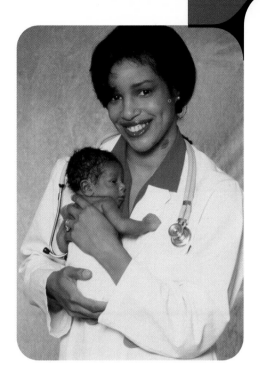

Kayeesha's dad had told her about the TV miniseries *Roots,*

which traces one person's African American background. She wanted to see it. When a local TV station aired *Roots* again in the 1990s, Kayeesha watched each episode.

"The violence and pain in *Roots* blew me away," she explained to her friend Dayla. "It seemed real and honest. I learned a lot about the strength and courage of my ancestors. I feel proud, and I want to learn more."

"Did it make you angry at white people?" asked Dayla.

"No. That's in the past," Kayeesha replied. "Most white people today aren't so narrow minded. You're white, and you don't treat me differently than you do anyone else."

Psychologist Edward Donnerstein believes some violence can be positive. For example, a police officer in a TV show may shoot someone and end up in counseling. That sends a different message from a program that shows only the shooting.

Not All Violence Is the Same

Some violence shown in the media can oppose actual violence. It does this by showing how violence negatively affects the victim, witness, and the perpetrator. This is a person who commits a crime. For example, the movie *Glory* is about an all-black regiment in the Civil War. Through several realistic scenes, viewers see the results of violence on the film's characters.

News coverage of war can serve the same purpose. Viewers get a glimpse of destroyed homes and suffering people. The pain and death of both victims and perpetrators are clear. When people see the outcome of violent activity, they may think twice before using violence.

Helping Law Enforcement

In cases of missing children, the media can help by providing film and photo coverage. For example, from 1984 to 1993, TV helped find 17,300 of 28,000 missing or sexually abused children. This resulted in putting more than 80 abusers or kidnappers on trial.

The media also have helped in arresting and convicting other criminals. For example, since 1998, *America's Most Wanted* has aided in capturing about 600 criminals.

Giving Positive Messages

In many cases, TV and films give positive messages. They show many examples of successful alternative families. Some programs demonstrate ways that teens have dealt successfully with peer pressure and depression. Many films, TV series, and specials offer examples of positive role models of various races.

Public service announcements provide other positive messages. They often feature celebrities. They may carry messages about avoiding drugs or building self-esteem, for instance.

Educating

Educational programs on TV help young people in many different ways. For example, *Sesame Street* and *Big Comfy Couch* have given children an early start at reading and social skills. *3-2-1 Contact* and *Bill Nye the Science Guy* have helped children learn and enjoy science. *Feeling Good* has helped improve health behaviors. *Mister Rogers' Neighborhood* uses entertainment to educate children. It teaches about cooperation, understanding others' feelings, and controlling aggression.

Points to Consider

Can you name three TV programs or movies that give positive messages? Explain the message of each and how it is shown.

What are some social concerns that TV or films have addressed?

Do you think violence in the media can be positive? Explain.

Do you think realistic violence is good or bad? Explain.

Chapter Overview

Some people have criticized TV news coverage for its violent content.

Some local stations attract viewers and sponsors through sensational news coverage.

Some stations have been successful by showing less violence.

Chapter **4**

Is Violence "Good News"?

Maggie is a good student. She
loves reading, particularly current

MAGGIE, AGE 13

events. She reads the newspaper every day and often buys
news and current events magazines. Maggie has wanted to go
into politics for as long as she can remember. One morning
Maggie surprised her parents. She announced that she was no
longer going to watch the nightly news. "I have bad dreams,
and I often wake up crying," Maggie said. "All of those stories
and film clips of people hurting one another make me feel
terrible. Maybe instead of becoming a U.S. Senator I will go
and live in another country," she added.

News Programs

Some people believe that local news programs are too violent. Some people think these programs are more violent than even police shows or movies about killers. The use of violence in news programs brings many questions to mind. Does violence make good news? Why are so many news stories about crime? Are stories that show people helping others less interesting than stories that show people hurting other people? How much of the news is accurate and how much of it is sensational? That is, how much news contains graphic words or pictures just to get a strong response from viewers?

There is a slogan rumored to be popular among news stations: "If it bleeds, it leads." According to the slogan, bloody, violent crime should appear at the beginning of the news. People who believe these words may feel that this approach works best to get and keep viewers. As more people watch such news, more advertisers will use that station. Advertisers pay TV stations money to advertise between news stories. That money is a powerful reason for stations to keep doing what they are doing.

ROBERTO, AGE 16

Roberto's brother, Emilio, was killed during a robbery in a convenience store. Emilio was simply in the store getting milk. One of the robber's bullets hit and killed Emilio.

Roberto, his mother, and his father saw a news story about Emilio's murder. The video showed Emilio's body lying in a pool of blood in the store aisle. The news station showed the video again after the police caught the robber.

Roberto thinks it's wrong for TV news people to make a family suffer even more. Why did the robbery have to be shown on TV? Why did they show Emilio's body and make his mother cry even harder?

Focus on Crime

Focusing on violence seems to work for some TV stations. For example, in the early 1990s, one Miami TV station, WSVN, decided to focus on violent crime. Many of the station's news programs led with graphic pictures of violent events. Some people criticized this trend toward sensational news. However, the station's number of viewers and amount of money from advertisers soared. Seeing this success, many other stations around the United States decided to show more violence, too.

Brief news flashes may give viewers an idea of violent activity. However, these short items may not show the harm that violence causes a victim. They may not show the pain and suffering of the victim's loved ones and witnesses. They may not show the regret or sadness of the person who caused the violence.

During the programming changes at WSVN, viewers were surveyed. About 7 out of 10 people in South Florida said that local news frightened them. However, many people continued to watch. People's fear grew even though the actual crime rate in Florida was decreasing at that time.

A Different Kind of Success

After receiving complaints about violence, KVUE, a TV station in Austin, Texas, decided to try an experiment. Station executives believed violent stories did not have to lead a news program. Sometimes these stories could be used within the news program instead. Limiting the video of victims, weapons, or perpetrators also could reduce the violence in the news. KVUE created these five standards for whether the station should show a story:

Does some action need to be taken about this story?

Is there an immediate threat to public safety?

Is there a specific threat to children?

Will the story affect the community?

Does the story lend itself to crime prevention?

The public reacted positively to KVUE's programming choices. Some other local stations showed as much violence as they ever did. However, KVUE offered an alternative for viewers in Austin.

Points to Consider

Do you think most people are likely to watch the news if it contains violence? Why or why not?

How has a specific violent news story affected you? Explain.

If you were the producer of a news program, how would you treat violent events?

Chapter Overview

Some films have been linked to violent behavior.

Saturday morning children's TV has 20 to 25 acts of violence per hour. Many children's cartoons are among the most violent programs on TV.

Media violence appears to affect other countries besides the United States and Canada.

Chapter 5

Film and TV Violence

Tomas grew up watching action movies. He believed that the strongest men were the best men. Tomas used to fight as much as any big-screen star. No one would ever take advantage of him. Tomas seriously hurt the last boy he fought. Now at age 15, Tomas is in a juvenile detention center for at least two years.

Tomas's mom used to say, "Can't you work things out by talking with other kids instead of fighting?"

Tomas used to tell her, "Talking doesn't do any good when you disagree. Guys in movies don't compromise." Now, however, he wishes he had tried talking instead of fighting.

Violence in Films

Several violent real-life incidents have been linked to films. Whether these movies actually influenced people's actions is not clear.

For example, in 1997, a 14-year-old boy in Paducah, Kentucky, shot eight fellow students. The boy claimed that the movie *The Basketball Diaries* influenced him. The central character in the movie dreams that he shoots classmates and teachers.

In April 1999, two students in Littleton, Colorado, killed 13 people and wounded dozens of others. Then they killed themselves. The *New York Post* compared the event to *The Basketball Diaries*. Its main character wears a black trench coat similar to the kind that the Littleton killers wore. However, in their taped confession, the killers say they thought of the shooting on their own. As a result of these and other incidents, no more video copies of the film have been produced.

A 1994 incident in Kentucky was linked to the film *Menace II Society*. Teens killed one boy and wounded another after running their car off the road. Some people said this incident was patterned on an incident in that film.

The National TV Violence Study took place during the mid-1990s. Results of this study showed that about 60 percent of TV programming contained some violence. Attractive characters committed 40 percent of violent crimes. Seventy-five percent of violent acts went unpunished. More than half of these acts did not show the suffering of victims.

Violence on Children's Programs

Saturday morning network children's programming is more violent than prime time TV. Prime time TV has 3 to 5 violent acts per hour. Saturday morning shows have 20 to 25 violent acts per hour.

The Mighty Morphin Power Rangers, for example, has been considered one of the most violent children's programs. The show makes killing look fun as perpetrators laugh and joke about it. Victims may be burned to death, blown apart, strangled, dismembered, or zapped by fancy weapons. This program violated Canada's TV broadcast code. As a result, the program was changed and, in some cases, canceled.

The cartoon characters Beavis and Butt-head torture animals, bother girls, and sniff, or smell, paint thinner. The two boys also often played with fire in the show. One mother said this led her five-year-old son to set fire to his home, killing his sister. Since that time, producers of the show have kept the characters from engaging in such behavior.

A Worldwide Effect

Violence appears in North American media. However, it is not limited to North America. Media violence seems to be a problem all over the world.

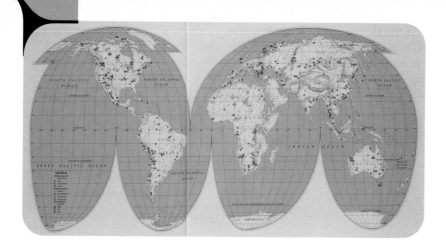

The United Nations Educational, Scientific, and Cultural Organization (UNESCO) conducted the Global Study on Media Violence. The study shows that media violence affects people everywhere in similar ways. In this study, 5,000 12-year-olds from 23 countries answered survey questions. These young people live in Africa, Asia, Europe, and North and South America. Some of the young people are from violent areas of big cities. Some are from areas without much violence. Almost half of the kids thought that what they saw on TV looked like real life. Nearly half said that they felt anxious about their life either most of the time or very often.

Points to Consider

If you were a TV producer, what would you do to limit violence in your TV programs?

Do you think children's cartoons are too violent? Why or why not?

Have you ever seen violence on the screen that disturbed you? What caused your reaction?

In your opinion, are some people likely to copy violence they see on the screen? Why or why not?

Chapter Overview

Many modern music lyrics are filled with violent images.

Some heavy metal music contains messages of hate against minority groups. Some acts of violence have been linked to this kind of music.

Some kinds of rap seem to encourage violence.

Studies show that violence in video games affects people negatively.

Chapter 6

Violence in Music and Video Games

LaMonte loved many kinds of heavy metal and rap music. His girlfriend, Sindee, put up with it for a while.

LAMONTE AND SINDEE, AGE 17

Sometimes when LaMonte was listening to music he would sing the words to Sindee. One time he called her his "nasty bitch" as he sang along to a song.

Sindee decided that she had had enough. She was no one's "nasty bitch." She told LaMonte his behavior bothered her. Sindee asked him how he would like it if someone called him names like that. Now LaMonte is more sensitive when he and Sindee listen to music he likes.

In 1957, *The Ed Sullivan Show* pictured singer Elvis Presley only above the waist. The producers considered Presley's dancing too sexual.

Concerns About Music

Concerns about music are not a recent problem. For example, in the 1950s, some parents worried about how the new rhythms of rock music would affect their children. In the 1960s, some parents disliked the long hair many singers had. Many parents reacted to song words that described drug use.

Like much current music, the words of popular music in the past dealt with rebelling against authority. However, some kinds of modern music frequently mention violence against women, oneself, or other groups of people.

Messages of Heavy Metal Music

Heavy metal music is energetic and highly amplified electronic rock music with a hard beat. Heavy metal songs often have lyrics, or words, that are sexist, racist, and violent. For example, one song offers an explanation for killing a girlfriend with a knife: "Killing you helped me keep you home." Another song puts down African Americans and immigrants. It also puts down gay and lesbian people, who are attracted to or sexually involved with someone of their own gender.

Violent Events and Heavy Metal Music

Promoting hatred may not be physically violent. However, the effects of promoting hatred can be. For example, in one heavy metal music video, a father scolds his son for listening to rock music. The son, in turn, throws his father through a plate glass window. Some people believe this video inspired a New Mexico teen who murdered his father in a similar way.

A knapsack filled with heavy metal videos was found at a murder site in Los Angeles. Along with it was a baseball cap with a heavy metal band's logo. Some people believe a heavy metal song about someone who prowls at night inspired the killer.

Suicide

It's not easy to be a teen. Many teens have problems dealing with school or personal relationships with parents or others. They may be afraid or confused about the future. These problems may contribute to feeling hopeless or depressed. Untreated depression is the leading cause of teen suicide, which is killing oneself. Suicide is the third leading cause of death among teens.

Some modern music seems to encourage suicide. For example, two 15-year-old girls left a suicide note that quoted the lyrics to a heavy metal song. In another example, a young man killed himself while listening to a heavy metal song about suicide. However, the singer of the song said that it was about his own depression and suicidal thoughts. He wrote it to express how he felt, not to encourage others to commit suicide.

Satanism

Some heavy metal bands write lyrics about devil worship, also called satanism. This kind of activity sometimes involves violence and even murder. Evidence of heavy metal music is found in 35 to 40 percent of crime scenes involving satanism. For instance, a devil-worshiping religious group in New York killed a man during a ritual killing. The group left behind the names of heavy metal bands that have sung about Satan taking over someone's body.

Feelings about ragtime music were strong around 1900. The American Federation of Musicians passed a resolution urging its members to "make every effort to suppress such musical trash."

Rap Music

Rap started in the 1980s in U.S. urban areas. Many rap songs were originally about social issues that were important to their audiences. Over time, "gangsta rap" came into being. It often makes the life of criminals look attractive. Many gangsta rap songs contain lyrics that are violent and sexist. For instance, a 1992 song encouraged the killing of police. Law enforcement and citizens' groups asked people not to buy the record.

Rap songs sometimes describe females as males' playthings. For instance, one such song is about a machine that automatically hits a female until she obeys. Videos that accompany rap songs often show males ruling and controlling females.

Violence in Video Games

Children spend more time playing video games today than ever before. Many of these games may be a fun challenge, but many have violent themes. Fewer studies are available on video game violence than there are on TV violence. However, early studies show that violent games seem to have a negative effect, especially on children.

For example, Eric Harris was one of the teens who shot students and a teacher in Littleton, Colorado. In videotapes of the preparation for the school shooting, Harris sits with a sawed-off shotgun in his lap. Harris calls the weapon Arlene, after a character in the *Doom* video game. He also said that the killing was going to be just like *Doom*.

Michael Carneal shot fellow students in West Paducah, Kentucky. He became good at using a gun because he practiced so much with point-and-shoot video games.

Points to Consider

Why do you think songwriters use lyrics that may offend some people?

Do you think songs inspire people to commit acts such as suicide or murder? Why or why not?

Do you think gangsta rap encourages violence? Why or why not?

Do you think violent video games affect the people who play them? Who might be most affected? Explain.

Chapter Overview

The V-Chip helps parents to decide on suitable TV programming for their children.

TV programmers have volunteered to rate all programming except for news, sporting events, and emergency broadcasts.

Many people in media industries are working to decrease children's exposure to violence.

Women and men can act to change the amount of violence in the media.

You can influence the media positively.

Chapter 7

Dealing With Media Violence

MARTIN, AGE 16

While baby-sitting his sister, Sara, Martin invited some friends over to watch *Murder by Power Tool*. Sara wanted to watch, too, but Martin sent her to bed. When he turned to the movie, the message "This program exceeds your rating limit" ran across the screen. Martin was angry. His parents were using the V-Chip again.

"My friends and I wanted to watch a movie last night, Mom. But the V-Chip ruined that idea," Martin angrily told his mother.

"Sorry, Martin," his mom said. "I know you can handle the violence, but I don't want Sarah to see or hear that stuff."

In 1998, two-thirds of adults surveyed said they would not buy a V-Chip box. They wouldn't buy a new TV simply because it contained the V-Chip. If the adults already had a TV with a V-Chip, however, two-thirds of them said they would use it.

The V-Chip

In February 1996, U.S. President Bill Clinton signed the Telecommunications Act. Part of this law called for the manufacture of the V-Chip, a computer microprocessor. Parents and other concerned adults can use this computer processor to screen TV programs. It is meant as a tool to help caregivers guide their children's TV watching. TVs containing the V-Chip became available during the fall of 1996.

By mid-1998, a box equipped with the V-Chip was introduced. This box is made for older TV sets built without a V-Chip. This product resembles a cable box and costs between $80 and $100.

Starting in January 2000, all new TVs with screens larger than 13 inches will have the V-Chip. Many TV sets produced in 1999 already contained the V-Chip.

The V-Chip Process

The V-Chip process begins when broadcasters air a TV program or movie. Most programs receive a ratings signal that is broadcast with them. The V-Chip compares this signal to preselected limits. If the program rating is higher than the limit, the chip does not allow the program to come through. Instead, the screen remains blank. A program's rating appears on screen for the first 15 seconds of a show.

Most TV programs are rated according to the TV Parental Guidelines System. The National Association of Broadcasters, the National Cable TV Association, and the Motion Picture Association of America created this rating system. Broadcast signals are based on these ratings. News, sporting events, and emergency broadcast signals are not rated. Therefore, the V-Chip does not block them.

A Meeting With Hollywood

In the mid-1990s, a group from the U.S. Congress met with Hollywood producers of film and TV programming. More than half of these producers agreed that violence in the media is a problem. Nearly 9 out of 10 of them believe that media violence contributes to real violence. Two-thirds of these media professionals felt that the media make violence look attractive.

The Children's Television Act

In 1990, the U.S. Congress passed the Children's Television Act. This law requires broadcasters to provide programs that educate and inform children. However, later research showed that many stations weren't providing as much educational programming as expected.

MTV now rejects one out of four music videos submitted to it because of strong violent or sexual content.

People Reacting to Violence in the Media

Members of the public have placed pressure on producers. As a result:

Violence experts will help networks to create less violent storylines.

Network and cable producers will use unbiased groups to track TV violence.

Children's programmers will add more educational shows.

Programs that contain violence will air later in the evening. That is a time when young children are less likely to watch.

Many people believe that TV, movies, music, and video games show people as stereotypes. For example, women are often stereotyped as things for men to use. Many groups work for controls and changes in these media. Letter-writing campaigns to complain about TV ads have had some positive results. Some companies are learning that people won't accept the use of sexuality in advertising or entertainment.

Some men's and women's groups have protested against certain kinds of music. These groups believe that many popular songs describe females as males' property. The protests have taken many forms. For example, Operation PUSH (People United to Save Humanity) has asked people not to buy music that puts down females.

Some entertainers, such as Queen Latifah, perform a counter rap that is intended to be constructive. This rap does not include the violence that some rap does. It refers to females as strong individuals.

Sega of America and David Walsh of the Johnson Institute now rate video games. These ratings are meant to aid parents and other adults in deciding which games are suitable for children.

What You Can Do

You can do several things to help influence the media in a positive way.

If you see a violent TV program or film with someone else, talk about it. Talk about the causes and the consequences of the violence. Consider peaceful alternatives to violence.

If a child you know wants to watch TV, encourage him or her to read a book instead.

You may not like some violence you see in the media. In that case, write a letter to the producer of the program or its advertisers. Tell them specifically what you didn't like.

Organize a letter-writing campaign if you believe some media presentation was particularly harmful.

Friends may try to talk you into seeing a violent movie. If you feel the movie is too violent, don't give in and go. Compromise and see something everyone can be comfortable with.

Object to any media that encourage hate toward any group.

Cecily baby-sits part time for her Aunt Felicia's three kids. It's tough at times, but she does like those kids.

One day, Cecily and the kids watched a TV drama. In it, a drunk driver killed the parents of two small children. Cecily was surprised at how negatively her aunt's children reacted.

The program gave Cecily a chance to talk with the kids about drinking and driving. She talked with them about how easy it is for careless people to hurt others. Cecily and the kids also talked about ways to be good neighbors.

Points to Consider

Do you think the V-Chip is effective? Why or why not?

What are networks doing to prevent children from seeing too much violence? Do you think their efforts work? Why or why not?

Do you think more action needs to be taken against media violence? Why or why not?

How can you help children to avoid the negative effects of TV violence?

Glossary

censor (SEN-sur)—to remove content because some people object to it

desensitize (dee-SEN-suh-tize)—to make less affected by something, such as pain or hardship

empathy (EM-puh-thee)—the ability to understand how something such as excitement, fear, or pain affects someone else

Holocaust (HOL-uh-kost)—the murder of Jews and others during World War II

mass media (MASS MEE-dee-uh)—forms of media that can reach many people at the same time

media (MEE-de-uh)—films, TV, radio, videotapes, video games, and printed materials

microprocessor (MYE-kroh-pross-ess-ur)—a tiny computer chip

moral code (MOH-ruhl KODE)—a clear sense of right and wrong

outcry (OUT-krye)—a loud complaint about something

perpetrator (PUR-puh-trayt-ur)—someone who commits a crime

prime time (PRIME TIME)—the time period when the most people watch TV; prime time is usually in the evening.

sensational (sen-SAY-shuhn-uhl)—news full of graphic words or pictures just to get a strong response

stereotype (STER-ee-oh-tipe)—an overly simple idea or opinion of a person, group, or thing

unprotected sex (uhn-pruh-TEK-tuhd SEKS)—sexual behavior that isn't protected against unintended pregnancy or disease

For More Information

Day, Nancy. *Sensational TV: Trash or Journalism?* Springfield, NJ: Enslow, 1996.

Dudley, William, ed. *Media Violence: Opposing Viewpoints.* San Diego: Greenhaven, 1999.

Gedatus, Gus. *Violence in Public Places.* Mankato, MN: Capstone: 2000.

Gedatus, Gus. *Violence in School.* Mankato, MN: Capstone: 2000.

McGuckin, Frank, ed. *Violence in American Society.* New York: H. W. Wilson, 1997.

Useful Addresses and Internet Sites

Center for Violence and Injury Prevention
Education Development Center, Inc.
55 Chapel Street
Newton, MA 02458
www.edc.org

National Center for Injury Prevention and
Control
Division of Violence Prevention
Mailstop K60
4770 Buford Highway Northeast
Atlanta, GA 30341-3724
www.cdc.gov/ncipc

National Crime Prevention Council
1700 K Street Northwest, 2nd Floor
Washington, DC 20006-3817
www.ncpc.org/1safe6dc.htm

Office of Juvenile Justice and Delinquency
Juvenile Justice Clearing House
PO Box 6000
Rockville, MD 20849-6000
1-800-638-8736

Early Childhood/Teen Communications Project
http://depts.washington.edu/ecttp/
 violence/v2.html
Information on the media's effect on teens,
provides an example, and posts feedback from
teens reacting to the example

Media Awareness Network (Canada)
www.media-awareness.ca/eng
Information about media awareness for
teachers, parents, and the general public plus
information about what the Canadian
government has done regarding violence in the
media

Media Literacy Online Project
http://interact.uoregon.edu/MediaLit/FA/
 articles/violence.html
Links to information on violence, sex, and
media

National Coalition on Television Violence
www.nctvv.org
Information about violence in the media,
action communities can take, and letter-writing
samples and addresses to voice opinions
against violence

National Institute on Media and the Family
www.mediaandthefamily.com
Resources for research, information, and
education on the effects of media on children
and families

Index

advertisers, 32, 33, 56, 58

Beavis and Butt-head, 41
books, 6, 58

Canadian Broadcaster's Association, 11
Canadian Radio-television and
    Telecommunications
    Commission (CRTC), 11
censorship, 12
Charter of Rights and Freedoms, 12
children
    programs for, 28–29, 40–41
    and violence in the media, 15–17,
      53, 55, 59
Children's Television Act, 55
counselors, 20

depression, 20
Doom, 50

educating viewers, 17, 19, 24, 26,
    28–29, 55, 59
emotions, 5, 10, 17, 20, 25, 31, 34, 42

females, 19, 24, 45, 49, 56–57
films, 6, 7, 8, 15, 24, 26, 38–39
    influence of, 7, 16–17, 19, 37–39
    positive effects and images in,
      24–28
    rating system of, 8–9, 12
    violence in, 5, 8–10, 15–17, 20, 24,
      26, 37, 38–39
First Amendment, 10, 12
Franklin, Benjamin, 6

gangsta rap, 45, 49

KVUE, 34–35

hatred, 46, 47, 48, 49, 58
heavy metal music, 46–48

imagination, 6

law enforcement, 27, 49
letter-writing campaign, 58

males, 19–20, 37, 49, 56–57
mass media. *See* films; media; music,
    recorded; TV; video games
media
    history, 5, 8–10, 46
    influence of the, 6–7, 15–19,
      37–39, 41, 47–49, 50
    influencing the, 56–57, 58–59
    negative ideas and messages
      portrayed in, 15–21, 46–49
    positive effects and images of,
      23–29
    violence, 5, 8–11, 16–20, 31–34,
      37–42, 45–50, 53, 55, 59
monitoring, 11, 12
Motion Picture Association of America
    (MPAA), 8, 55
movies. *See* films
MTV, 56
music, recorded, 6, 12, 45–49, 57
    heavy metal, 46–48
    influence of, 47–49
    rap, 45, 49, 57

Index continued

National Association of Broadcasters, 55

National Cable TV Association, 55

news programs, 10, 26, 31–35

Operation PUSH, 57

point-and-shoot video games, 50

prejudice, 46, 47, 49

prime time, 10, 40

public service announcements, 27

Queen Latifah, 57

radio, 6, 7

ragtime music, 49

rap music, 45, 49, 57

rating systems, 8–9, 11, 12, 40, 53, 54–55, 57

role models, 19–20, 23, 25, 27

satanism, 48

sensationalism, 32, 33

sexism, 45, 46, 49, 57

sexual intercourse, 18

Shakespeare, William, 6

soap operas, 18

stereotypes, 19–20, 37, 49, 56
    breaking down, 23

suicide, 47–48

Telecommunications Act, 54

TV, 6
    children's programs, 28–29, 40–41, 55

educational programs, 28–29, 55

and false view of the world, 17–19

influence of, 15–19, 41

news programs, 10, 26, 31–35

positive effects and images on, 23–28

rating system of, 11, 12, 40, 53, 54–55

and the V-chip, 53, 54–55

violence on, 8–11, 15–17, 18, 20, 24, 32–34, 40–41

TV shows, 7, 18, 23, 25, 27, 28, 29

United Nations Educational, Scientific, and Cultural Organization (UNESCO), 42

U.S. Congress, 10, 55

V-chip, 53, 54–55

video games, 6, 12, 50, 57

videotapes, 6, 39, 47

violent behavior, 15–17, 18, 20, 37–42, 48–50

war, 5, 24, 26

world views of media violence, 41–42

WSVN, 33–34